If MY People . . .

D1473840

Wayne C. & Stephanie Anderson

If MY People . . .

ISBN: 9798833728918
Imprint: Independently published

If MY People . . .

If My People . . .

The responsibility of a nation in peril belongs to His people and not politicians or the media or any consortium of wealthy plutocrats.

His people, however strong or weak in their uniqueness, they may seem, hold the true destiny of a nation in their hands. When His people call out to Him, He heals.

There is a mystery yet to be unfolded about how Yehovah heals the land and thus heals the people of the land. We talk more about this mystery on our podcasts: Standsure.net/mypeople

If MY People . . .

If MY People . . .

CONTENTS

Table of Contents

If MY People . . .

The healing of your land, in whatever nation you abide, comes when those who have His name called upon them will humble themselves and pray.

This does not require cooperation with anyone except you and the Holy One. Cooperation, collaboration, or teamwork is great but is no excuse to rule out your participation.

If you are His, your uniqueness is a strength, and the deliverance of the nation depends upon you. This is because you have been born for just such a time as this.

If MY People . . .

Introduction

*"Why do nations assemble, and peoples
plot vain things, kings of the earth take
their stand, and regents intrigue together
against the LORD {Yehovah}
and against His anointed?
'Let us break the cords of their yoke,
shake off their ropes from us!'
He who is enthroned in heaven laughs;
the Lord mocks at them."*
Psalms 2:1-4 (Tanakh)

The days in which we now live are
written in heaven's scrolls.

Billionaires control the governments of
the entire planet. Unfortunately, we, the
people, have become the pawns in their

1

games of control and manipulations.

The entire world changed on the eleventh day of September 2001, as we entered the twenty-first century - the new millennium. The happenings from that point on are stranger than fiction.

Plandemics are now coming in waves with no hope of an end. Useless masks have become badges of honor to those who have given themselves to the slavery of the system. Revolutions and civil wars are looming. Irreconcilable differences in standing belief systems are sure to tear nations apart.

The global church stands in fear, pride, ego, vanity, and assumption, and leadership has little faith. There is too much hiding and wringing of the hands. While theology divides and weakens ny unifying power of the people with 'th, there exists a people who know d and not just about Him. At the same ', theology has made its own rules, od lovers are personally involved he Master of the Universe. bers matter little. The intensity of the Creator and love for one · will triumph, and there is no

2

evidence to say otherwise.

The scroll is clear, concise, and understandable:

"If My people who are called by My name {literally: "over whom My name is called"} will humble themselves, and pray and seek My face, and turn from their wicked ways, then I will hear from heaven, and will forgive their sin and heal their land. Now My eyes will be open, and My ears attentive to the prayer of this place. For now, I have chosen and sanctified this house, that My name may be there forever, and My eyes and My heart will be there perpetually."
2 Chronicles 7:14-16

Messiah Christ Jesus says it this way, *"And whatever you ask in My name, that I will do, that the Father may be glorified in the Son. If you ask anything in My name, I will do it."*
John 14:13-14

There is a move of God taking place, and the hosts of heaven respond to the faith found upon the earth. Faith in the

Name. Submersed in the Name.

The world will not - cannot repent. Only His people who have His Name called upon them can repent. The land will hear the voice of the Creator and will respond to His will.

> *". . . 'Men and brethren,*
> *what shall we do?'*
> *Peter said to them,*
> *'Repent, and let every one of you be*
> *baptized in the name of Jesus Christ for*
> *the remission of sins; and you shall*
> *receive the gift of the Holy Spirit.*
> *For the promise is to you, your children,*
> *and all who are afar off, as many as the*
> *Lord our God will call.'*
> *And with many other words,*
> *he testified and exhorted them,*
> *saying, 'Be saved from*
> *this perverse generation.'"*
> Acts 2:37-40

"Come Kingdom of God! Be done will of God! On earth as in heaven!"

"I Saw Three Men . . ."

"I Saw Three Men . . ."

It was a beautiful late spring day on our ranch in the western foothills of the Rockies. I (Wayne) was home alone and had been working on a fencing project in the pasture and an electrical project on the barn. But, since my early morning coffee, I'd been working outside and enjoying the Presence of the Lord and having loving conversations with the One Who loved me first.

By mid-morning, I required a unique fence repairing tool in our home's garage. So, I walked across the front of the property, opened the garage doors, and headed into the garage to hunt for the

5

needed tool.

I came out of the garage to walk back with the tool to where I was working, and to my surprise, I saw three men walking down the driveway toward me. At least one seemed to have a clipboard with papers, and one had a measuring device.

I walked about ten steps to the house's front porch to set the rather bulky tool down to converse with the men properly. As I turned back around, the three men were not there. As I glanced around to try and find where they went in those few seconds, I could see clearly around them for more than a thousand feet. Either they had disappeared into thin air, or I was completely mistaken. Or was it a vision?

I turned and picked up the tool and went back to work, asking the Holy One what happened. I felt that the vision was for a purpose and began to deliberate upon what the vision might mean. Soon I forgot about it as I finished the fence work and started the electrical.

After taking apart some electrical pieces, I realized I needed my electrical toolbox in the garage. So, I walked across the front of the property again and entered the garage to fetch my toolbox. The three men were coming down the driveway again when I came out. Without thinking, I turned and set the toolbox down on the front porch and turned back to greet the men, only to find that they had disappeared again.

I sat down on the front porch and said, "Here am I, Lord. Please teach me." I remembered the scriptures describing the three men who came to Abraham when he was at the Oaks of Mamre. I opened the Bible program on my phone, poured through the scriptures, and found what the Holy One was teaching me.

The incident was in the late spring-early summer of 2009, at the beginning of Obama's crusade to destroy the world as we know it.

We've come a long way since the early Obama days, and the indignant sin of the billionaire club and the governments of every nation has closed in on the world's population. More than a decade later, the harbingers of scripture and history are blaring statements of judgment and condemnation.

Abraham's Intercession

*"Now the LORD appeared to him
by the oaks of Mamre while he
was sitting at the tent door in the
heat of the day. When he lifted up
his eyes and looked, behold,
three men were standing opposite him;
and when he saw them,
he ran from the tent door to meet
them and bowed himself to the
earth and said, "My Lord,
if now I have found favor
in Your sight, please
do not pass Your servant by."*
Genesis 18:1-3 (NASB)

*"And the LORD said,
'Because the outcry against
Sodom and Gomorrah is great,
and because their sin is very grave...'"*
Genesis 18:20 (NKJV)

"Abraham came near and said, 'Would You also destroy the righteous with the wicked? Suppose there were fifty righteous within the city; would You also destroy the place and not spare it for the fifty righteous that were in it? Far be it from You to do such a thing as this, to slay the righteous with the wicked, so that the righteous should be as the wicked; far be it from You! Shall not the Judge of all the earth do right?'
So the LORD said, 'If I find in Sodom fifty righteous within the city, then I will spare all the place for their sakes.'"
Genesis 18:23-26 (NKJV)

Abraham passionately and skillfully demonstrates the intricacies of intercession and the intercessory use of negotiations with Yehovah. As you read and study these scriptures, you'll find some exciting dialogue between Abraham and Yehovah. First, Abraham gets justice for 50 righteous people (if there be that many) in these city nations, then 45, 40, 30, 20, and finally 10.

The most crucial factor that we must understand is that the destruction of a nation, city, or land is not focused upon the evil but on the righteous who abide there.

Evil in a land draws the attention of heaven, and the Lord focuses on the land of His creation and judges the sin committed upon that land. (See Gen 4 Cain & Abel)

The plea for protection of the righteous in the land causes the wisdom of Yehovah to prevail on behalf of the righteous. Yet He will condemn the sin of the wicked spirits who cause the public to display evil.

The point we are making here is that the few righteous, who belong to Yehovah, have more say than the multitudes of persons under the controls of the "prince of the power of the air." These are those of "the spirit who now works in the sons of disobedience," who conduct themselves "in the lusts of the flesh, fulfilling the desires of the flesh and the mind, who are by nature children of wrath."[1]

The righteous have heaven's authority

---

[1] See Ephesians 2:1-3

and power in them. The righteous also have His promises to rely upon.

> *"Fear not, for I have redeemed you;*
> *I have called you by your name;*
> *you are Mine.*
>
> *When you pass through the waters, I will be with you; and through the rivers, they shall not overflow you. When you walk through the fire, you shall not be burned, nor shall the flame scorch you.*
>
> *I am the LORD {YHWH} your God, {Elohim}, the Holy One of Israel, your Savior; I gave Egypt for your ransom, Ethiopia and Seba in your place.*
>
> *Since you were precious in My sight, you have been honored, and I have loved you; Therefore, I will give men for you and people for your life.*
>
> *Fear not, for I am with you; I will bring your descendants from the east and gather you from the west;*

If MY People . . .

I will say to the north, 'Give them up!' And to the south, 'Do not keep them back!' Bring My sons from afar, and My daughters from the ends of the earth—

Everyone who is called by My name, whom I have created for My glory; I have formed him, yes, I have made him."
Isaiah 43:1-7 (NKJV)

Day of False Prophets?

Prophets see what will happen if . . .

Let's face it; no other generation of people has had information flow so inexhaustibly, randomly, and obscurely as the generation in which we live. It has come upon us and is growing upon us so rapidly that very small children are more capable of fixing our electronic gadgets than mature adults.

Like never before, we are able to hear messages from the prophets. Prophets from every continent hear and see the dooming harbingers of wickedness and its rewards. Every nation is in trouble. There is nowhere to run - nowhere to hide.

The future looks very bad if you listen to what the prophets say. But do we label them as "doomsday prophets" and not listen? Is it possible that they are simply doing their job announcing the will of heaven? There is nothing safe about plugging your ears to what prophets say about this adulterous, sinful and unbelieving generation.

In the synagogue of His hometown, Jesus prophesied, and they tried to throw Him off a cliff. He said, "No prophet is welcome in his hometown."

He then gave the examples of both Elijah & Elisha, who are arguably the most famous prophets of that society and beyond.

Of Elijah, Jesus says that there were "many widows in Israel in the days of Elijah." Yet the prophet was sent to "none of them, but only to Zarephath, in the land of Sidon, to a woman who was a widow."[2]

Later, Jesus conveys that "an evil and adulterous generation craves for a sign,

---

[2] Luke 4:24-26

yet no sign will be given to it but the sign of Jonah the prophet." The "sign of Jonah the prophet" is consequential amid a wicked generation.

In the gospels, Jesus uses the prophetic life of Jonah three times, and the name Jonah is used eight times by Him.[3]

Jesus refers to the Zarephath widow and Jonah in His prophetic proclamations of the signs of the times for an evil generation. To understand more of the depth of what He is saying, we need to know more about Jonah and what this sign could mean. Are the prophets of today a Jonah sign?

If we listen to what Jesus is saying, we must realize we live in an evil, adulterous, craving, wicked, and condemned generation, and there is judgment. His justice will prevail. In order to understand the victory given unto us, we need to understand more about Jonah, the prophet and preacher of whom Jesus speaks.

Then we can perhaps understand the

---

[3] Please read: Matthew 12:39-41, Matthew 16:2-4, Luke 11:29-32

"sign of Jonah" and what it means to us in this generation. What was the preaching of Jonah that we should hear?

First, let us investigate the history of Jonah, who he was, and what he preached? Jonah's beginnings are rather miraculous.

Jesus used the widow of Zarephath as a prophetic insult to the religious people of an evil generation. It nearly got Him thrown off a cliff.

"Now it came about after these things that the son of the woman, the mistress of the house, became sick, and his sickness was so severe that there was no breath left in him." - 1 Kings 17:17

According to scripture, the woman in Zarephath that Elijah went to was a widow. But, unfortunately, the child of this widow became ill and actually died. Yet "The LORD heard the voice of Elijah, and the life of the child returned to him, and he revived."[4]

We then find that Elijah took the child from the "upper room into the house and gave him to his mother." So, it's

---

[4] 1 Kings 17:22-24

reasonably safe to say that life-changing, world-changing things have Biblically happened in upper rooms.[5]

Jonah's life was a sign of resurrection power in an upper room. According to Jewish history and the Talmud, the boy that Elijah and Yehovah raised up from the dead in that upper room was Jonah, ben Amittai - son of truth.[6]

Midrash, Yerushalmi Makkos 2:6, says, "The son of the widow of Zarephath (Tzorfas), the child whom Elijah brought back to life, was Jonah. He was a complete tzaddik.[7]

Historically we find that Jonah's mother gave him to Elijah as one of the "sons of the prophet." When Elisha witnessed, "Elijah went up by a whirlwind to heaven," Jonah then came under the tutelage of Elisha.

Jewish history informs us that Jonah was one of the sons of the prophets that Elisha sent to anoint Jehu as king.[8]

One reason Jonah did not want to go

---

[5] i.e. Holy Ghost Pentecost, Passover Feast of Jesus
[6] Reference to: Midrash Shocher Tov 26:7
[7] tzaddik is a righteous human being
[8] 2 Kings 9

to Nineveh to prophesy their doom is that he had already done so in Jerusalem, and the people repented so that none of that which He predicted came to pass. He was accused of being a false prophet because of Yehovah's acts of mercy toward the repentant.

This adds an urgent prophetic strength to the proclamations of Jesus and His "sign of Jonah." Jonah was called upon to proclaim the condemning justice of heaven upon a land. Yet, the "sign of Jonah" has the secondary call of repentance that comes with it.

A teaching of the Midrash says:

"They asked Wisdom, 'What is the sinner's punishment?' It told them, 'Sinners - let them be pursued by (their) evil.' {Proverbs 13:21}

They asked Prophesy, 'What is the sinner's punishment?' It told them, 'The soul that sins - it shall die.' {Ezekiel 18:20}

They asked Torah, 'What is the sinner's punishment?' It told them, 'Let him bring a guilt-offering and gain atonement.'

They asked the Holy One, blessed be He, 'What is the sinner's punishment?'

He told them, 'Let him repent and gain atonement!'[9]

When repentance comes, the miracles begin. The land starts its healing process.

As preachers of grace and new covenant freedom, we believe we have a new covenant of love and mercy. However, we believe it to be heresy if one invalidates a believers need and ability to repent, apologize and seek forgives because of any new covenant grace theology. This thinking disables the heavenly endowments of the miracles of the apology and forgiveness.

Sinners sin unto the death that they are already surrounded by, and they need a Lamb to take the sin and death away. Believers sin, and it counts. But believers have the miracle-working power of an apology and the cleansing work of forgiveness.

Simply put, we need the *"sign of Jonah"* to come upon the land and the people of the land. Then, we must hear

---

[9] Midrash, Yerushalmi Makkos 2:6

the judgment and respond. Apology and repentance begin miraculous change as the land heals from the wounds of wickedness.

Thus, Prophets see what will happen if . . .

. . . if His people are not humbled and take action.

The day?

It's a Jonah Day!

If MY People . . .

2 Chronicles 7:14-16 (NKJV)

"If <u>My people</u> who are called by <u>My name</u> will humble themselves, and pray and seek <u>My face</u>, and turn from their wicked ways, then I will hear from heaven and will forgive their sin and heal their land. Now <u>My eyes</u> will be open and <u>My ears</u> attentive to prayer made in this place. For now I have chosen and sanctified this house, that <u>My name</u> may be there forever, and <u>My eyes</u> and <u>My heart</u> will be there perpetually."

- My People
- My Name
- My Face
- My Eyes

- My Ears
- My Name
- My Eyes
- My Heart

When we view this powerful scripture with all the possessiveness of Yehovah's words, there ought to be a sense of grasping the huge identity rush that says, "Hey! I belong to Him!"

We ought also to see His desire for us to be His people, to have His name upon us, to behold His face, to look into His eyes, to whisper loving things to Him, and to have His heart that is focused upon each of us. Even the forgiveness given has a sweetness to us when we behold how He has given Himself unto us.

As humans, we tend to always look for what we need to do. Yet, we are human beings, not human doings. When you have such promises, how hard is it to "be" humble, turn from your ways, and "be" His?

If we could see through the mists and behold the heavenly hosts that are being victorious now and the implications and impressions that those victories are making upon the nations of this world, we would react differently to the world's unintelligent and wanton antics. They build all they want upon the sands. And yet the Holy Storm from the heavens is coming upon all they have constructed. The wealth of the world's wickedness has been and continues to be stored up for the righteous.

What the world is doing can even be entertaining to the righteous. "He who sits in the heavens laughs, Yehovah scoffs at them."[10]

For us to grasp the power of this scripture in our New Covenant life and learn to apply it accordingly, we need to focus on the heart of the Father when He spoke it to king Solomon.

Let us behold the love factor of Yehovah loving His people. His people will be humble and be forgiven. Yehovah's children will walk in the

---

[10] Psalms 2:1-4: 1 Why are the nations in an uproar and the peoples devising a vain thing? 2 The kings of the earth take their stand and the rulers take counsel together against the LORD and against His Anointed, saying, 3 "Let us tear their fetters apart and cast away their cords from us!" 4 He who sits in the heavens laughs, Yehovah scoffs at them.

closeness of forgiveness, and His Spirit gives them life.

When walking in the Spirit – walking in forgiveness and vulnerability – we are firmly established in love. Love overpowers the need to be right. To think right, to act right, and to have our behavioral beliefs established as right drives us in the direction of religion away from the behavior of Jesus Christ. Love in and from His presence covers the wrong and gives life.

From the early chapter of this book, we learned that Abraham's intercession was for the righteous people, not those who produced a society of debauchery. Therefore, the rescue focus was on the people who belonged to Yehovah.

This pivotal verse in 2nd Chronicles is the voice of Yehovah Himself to king Solomon. "Yehovah appeared to Solomon by night," and singled out His people, who are called by His name. That is Yehovah's family and not all the rest of the world. We are again shown that the people of Yehovah's household are most important to Him.

The destiny of God's people was activated in the days of David and Solomon. Solomon is a derivative of the word shalom, and Solomon (Hebrew: Shlomo) is the son of David (Hebrew, meaning "beloved"). So when the Name Yod-Hey-Vav-Hey - Yehovah is called upon David and Solomon, a Kingdom destiny principle shifts into place and begins to operate from heaven to earth. Israel became the dominant world power.

Let's look at the phrase "called by My name" to see what it means and how it applies. The Hebrew alludes to His Name having been called upon His people. The same is true in Deuteronomy 28:10-12:

"All the peoples of the earth shall see that you have the name of Yehovah called upon you, and they shall fear you. Yehovah shall prosper you in goods, and in the fruit of your body, and in the fruit of your livestock, and in the fruit of your ground in the land which Yehovah swore to your fathers to give it to you. Yehovah shall open to you His good treasure, the heavens to give the rain to your land in its season, and to bless all the work of your hand."

Yehovah spoke clearly to Moses and told him to instruct Aaron and his sons to proclaim the blessing upon all of Israel's children.[11] It is made clear in the verse following that:

"They shall invoke My name on the sons of Israel, and I then will bless them."
Numbers 6:27

As we work to unfold this great mystery of His name, His family, and His righteous people, we find that Yehovah has completed the infrastructure of a complete life-giving household. This household is not just a dwelling structure, but a completed society known to a few as His Kingdom. As we learn in the book "The Mystery In ONE,"[12] we now have the Paradise in Eden. But this means to us as new covenant believers that we have an entire household operating with us.

This pivotal verse makes Yehovah's possession remarkably clear. We have highlighted the possessive of <u>My people</u>,

---

[11] Numbers 6:22-26
[12] The Mystery In ONE by Wayne C. & Stephanie Anderson, available Standsure.net/mystery

26

My name, My face, My eyes, My ears, My name, My eyes, and My heart. This all makes a strong statement about Yehovah's heart toward that which belongs to Him. A myriad of scriptures tell us who we are to Him. For, *"We are His workmanship, created in Christ Jesus for good works, which God prepared beforehand so that we would walk in them."*[13]

The apostle John the Beloved wrote, *"as many as received Him, to them He gave the authority* (exousia) *to become children of God, even to those who believe in His name, who were born, not of blood nor the will of the flesh nor the will of man, but of God."*[14]

Even Abraham's intercession includes those of us who place our faith in Christ. Abraham put his faith in Yehovah, which was reckoned to him as righteousness. *"They which are of faith, the same are the children of Abraham."*[15]

In the context of 2nd Chronicles 7:14-16, we find that something extraordinary

---

[13] Ephesians 2:10
[14] John 1:12-13
[15] Galatians 3:7 (KJV)

has taken place. In the prior verses, Solomon dedicates the finishing touches to the Temple of Yehovah and sacrifices thousands of animals that took decades to prepare. These animals were to be of a perfected bloodline. A sacrifice this big was prepared for months and maybe years before it could take place. Finally, Solomon was satisfied, had given his best, and retired to his room. The atmosphere suddenly changes, and the manifest presence of the Holy One to Whom Solomon sacrificed was standing in the room with him. Yehovah tells Solomon that Israel will be disloyal and bring poverty upon themselves. But the house consecrated by the sacrifice would give Israel the promise of redemption if they humble themselves.

Our new covenant life is not because of our sacrifices. On the contrary, we have the best of the promises given in 2nd Chronicles 7:14-16 through and because of the sacrifice of the Son of God.

Through the Blood of Jesus Christ, we are His people.

We agonize over the condition of the world. Every day we hear of new depths that the God-haters have gone to build an infrastructure for their wickedness to flourish.

"And why should we feel anger at the world? As if the world would notice!" – – Euripides[16]

For a very long time, religiously bound believers have said and even taught from a works mentality that we only need to get the world saved. The problem is then left as if this gospel of salvation is the answer, but nothing is done to see it happen.

What are we to do? Shall we stand in an open field, lift our hands, and wait for a rapture to rescue us? The prophets tell us that judgment is almost here. Can we somehow turn it around? Can God really save the nations in a day?

"If MY People" is an ownership statement with wonder-filled overtones of His household filled with His children. This was strengthened mightily when

---

[16] Euripides: Ancient Greek tragedian ca. 480 - 406, https://en.wikipedia.org/wiki/Euripides

Christ died and rose from the dead, then the Holy Ghost filled believers on that day of Pentecost and has been doing so ever since.

Believers are His people. His family that He wants to be fruitful and multiply and fill the earth. John the Beloved Apostle and father in the faith penned,

"My little children, I am writing these
things to you so that you may not sin.
And if anyone sins,
we have an Advocate with the Father,
Jesus Christ the righteous."
1 John 2:1 (NASB)

Prior to this scripture, John writes about how miraculous the confession of sin is and how confession brings forgiveness by our faith in the sacrifice of Jesus Christ.[17]

Our new covenant gives us the extraordinary gift of repentance and

---

[17] 1 John 1:7-10 (NASB) "If we walk in the Light as He Himself is in the Light, we have fellowship with one another, and the Blood of Jesus His Son cleanses us from all sin. If we say we have no sin, we are deceiving ourselves, and the truth is not in us. If we confess our sins, He is faithful and righteous to forgive us our sins and to cleanse us from all unrighteousness. If we say that we have not sinned, we make Him a liar, and His word is not in us."

forgiveness. But the effectiveness of the apology and forgiveness is heavily dependent upon relationship.

Let's look at the breakdown of our deliverance:

- If MY People
- Whom MY name is called upon (His Household/family
- Humble themselves
- Pray & seek MY Face
- Turn from their wicked ways
- I will hear from heaven
- I will forgive their sin
- And heal their land

Signs of the times:

"Behold, I am going to send you Elijah the prophet before the coming of the great and terrible day of the LORD. He will restore the hearts of the fathers to their children and the hearts of the children to their fathers so that I will not come and smite the land with a curse."
Malachi 4:5-6 (NASB)

If MY People . . .

Turning Back Wickedness

BELIEVERS ARE REPOSITIONED: FROM EARTH TO HEAVENLY PLACES

Begging God to do something is painful and a massive misunderstanding of the power given to the believer in the new covenant life. We are called to believe and reposition ourselves according to Jesus Christ's accomplishments. The price that He paid is too dear for us to deny Him the ability to connect with us on His level. Religion and false humility prohibit His life from working with us and demands that He work for us and we work for Him.

The heart's desire of the Holy Spirit is

to work "with" us.

We are beginning to see the results of the powerful delivering force of heaven. As we witness the body of Christ believing and praying, 2 Chronicles 7:14. Worlds will respond to the delivering forces of heaven. Why? Because we have repositioned ourselves to the high heavenly place "with" Christ Jesus – the:

"Author and Finisher of our faith, who for the joy that was set before Him endured the cross, despising the shame, and has sat down at the right hand of the throne of God."
Hebrews 12:2

In Ephesians 2, the apostle Paul repositions the ekklesia in Ephesus to their high place in Truth. This makes known to the believer that we do not pray from below in an earthy, begging manner. But we sit "with" Him in council in the heavens. From there, we proclaim His will to be done on earth as in heaven.

"And you were dead in your trespasses and sins, in which you formerly walked according to the course of this world,

according to the prince of the power of the air, of the spirit that is now working in the sons of disobedience. Among them, we, too, all formerly lived in the lusts of our flesh, indulging the desires of the flesh and of the mind, and were by nature children of wrath, even as the rest. But God, being rich in mercy, because of His great love with which He loved us, even when we were dead in our transgressions, made us alive together with Christ (by grace you have been saved) and raised us up with Him, and seated us with Him in the heavenly places in Christ Jesus,"
Ephesians 2:1-6 (NASB)

We have a high calling to be with Him. Positioned is a place of high faith.

THE SERPENT BEGUILED EVE

Yehovah tells Solomon in 2 Chronicles 7:14 that His people will fall away from Him through their sin.

Too often, people question whether the Master of all creation "allows" people go into a sinful life with shameful

behaviors. Yehovah tells Solomon that
Israel will become wicked in their ways
and defile the land. Since the Holy One
tells of this future behavior of His people,
the arguments begin about how He
knows and why He would want to let
that happen.

Yehovah is not in control, He is in
charge, and His power will trump the
power of the evil one. He was there when
Eve was hoodwinked into believing the
serpent's lies. He plans to destroy the
power of the malicious serpent code and
give grace to erase every effect of sin in a
person's life. Ephesians chapter two
clearly annunciates this fact.

The apostle Paul tells the Corinthian
Ekklesia of his great distrust in the
deceptive power of the serpent. He even
says that he has apostolic "fear"[18] that
they would allow the beguiler to rob
them of their pure and simple love of
Jesus.

*"I fear lest by any means, as the
serpent deceived Eve in his craftiness, so
your thoughts should be corrupted from*

---

[18] Greek word is "phobon" from which we also get the English term phobia.

the purity which is due to Christ."
2 Corinthians 11:3 (LITV)

From this, we can understand that knowing the threatening power of persuasive divination that wickedness creates, the people are apt to disconnect from the Holy One.

We disconnect from faithless deceptions as we open our hearts and humbly approach the possibility that we have been losing our connection with Jesus Christ and all He has done for us. We turn from the serpent's lies and works and reconnect and reposition ourselves with Jesus Christ in heavenly places.

A THIEF ON A CROSS WITH JESUS IS REPOSITIONED IN PARADISE RESTORED

"...This man has done nothing wrong."
And he was saying, "Jesus, remember me when You come in Your kingdom!" And He said to him, "Truly I say to you, today you shall be with Me in Paradise."
Luke 23:41-43 (NASB)

The thief on the cross with Jesus proclaimed His innocence. The innocence became the believer's identification with Him. The man who hung next to Him as a convicted sinner was expunged of all effects of sin and repositioned that day into Paradise restored by the Christ.

He identified with us by being severely punished by the serpent's evil because we were deceived into a life of sin. Yet, *"He was pierced through for our sins/transgressions."*

The iniquitous sins of the bloodline that carried the serpent code of evil power to convince us of lust-filled behaviors are powerfully destroyed by Him. For, *"He was crushed for our iniquities."*[19]

The satan condemned our behavior and celebrated his own victory falsely by disabling Elohim's substance of His Kingdom shalom to surround us. Finally, *"The condemnation of our shalom fell upon Him."*[20]

---

[19] Our forefathers Isaiah 53:5 iniquities [עָוֹן avon or עָווֹן avon - iniquity, guilt, punishment for iniquity
[20] Isaiah 53:5

All sickness, disease, plagues, and traumas that have come upon the human bodies are the manipulations of creation by the princes of darkness and wickedness. The satan has manipulated and exploited Elohim's creation by the influence of the deceptions of sin via "the lust of the flesh, and the lust of the eyes, and the boastful pride of life." But the triumph of Christ's body identifies with creation and triumphs over the evil spirits' orchestrations, and *"By His stripes/scourging we are healed."*[21]

The heavenly and perfect example of identification victory is found in Christ's supremacy at the cross at Golgotha.

The physical location of the hill scripturally known to us as Golgotha, the place of the skull, has nothing to do with the shape and appearance of the slope chosen to crucify the Master. But historically, it is the traditional place where the bones of Adam & Eve were located. Talmudic history records that Yehovah's angel led Shem & Melchizedek with the bones of the honored father and

---

[21] Isaiah 53:5

mother of humanity to the holy place marked for the burial of the treasured "First Adam's" bones.

Yehovah declared His pure justice unto Adam, saying, *"...Till you return to the ground because from it you were taken; for you are dust, and to dust, you shall return."*[22]

Golgotha was the holy ground where Adam and Eve returned to the dust from which they were made. The place where the crucifixion happened reveals to us that the Son of God - God's Lamb - took up and carried off the sins of rebellion of Eve and Adam.[23]

The Blood of the Son of God - Creator of all that exists - fell to the very dust that the first Adam returned to because he was taken by the serpent's beguilement and dwelt in sin instead of the Paradise with Yehovah.

---

[22] Genesis 3:19 (NASB)
[23] The Mystery In ONE book by Wayne & Stephanie Anderson, Amazon.com, Standsure.net/mystery

If MY People . . .

NEHEMIAH INTERVENES
FOR A NATION

The scrolls clearly witnessed to those who rebuilt Jerusalem and the temple after their many years of incarceration in Babylon. Identifying with the sins of their fathers/mothers was necessary, and they knew it well. Without the acknowledgment that Yehovah is triumphant over sin, there could be no healing for the land - no city of the great King - no temple to represent their relationship with the Holy One.

The scrolls informed Nehemiah that Yehovah spoke to king Solomon telling him that Yehovah's people would sin, defiling the land He had given them. The answer to the healing of their land was issued in 2 Chronicles 7:14.

When Nehemiah prays, he uses Yehovah's outline for healing their land.

*"When I heard these words,
I sat down and wept and mourned
for days, and I was fasting and
praying before the God of heaven.*

I said, 'I beseech You, O LORD[24] God[25]
of heaven[26], the great and
awesome God, who preserves the
covenant and lovingkindness
for those who love Him and keep His
commandments, let Your ear
now be attentive and Your eyes
open to hear the prayer of Your
servant which I am praying
before You now, day
and night, on behalf of the sons of
Israel Your servants, confessing
the sins of the sons of Israel
which we have
sinned against You; I and
my father's house have sinned.'"
Nehemiah 1: 4-6

Just as in Yehovah's dialogue with
Solomon, Nehemiah appeals to Yehovah
by His name and position - Yehovah,
Elohim in the heavens. He also petitions
Him to both hear and see (as with His

---

[24] יהוה YHVH, i.e., יְהֹוָה - Yehovah, the proper name of the God of Israel
[25] אֱלֹהִים Elohim, - plural form God
[26] This word in Hebrew is שָׁמַיִם shamayim;- heaven, sky. This is a positioning word. The New Covenant positioning for the believer is this heavenly place. See Ephesians 2:6 "Raised us up together and seated us together in the heavenlies in Christ Jesus."

ears & eyes). Nehemiah's faith was strong in Yehovah's love for His people and His desire to hear them and see them.

Nehemiah then identifies with the iniquitous sins of his fathers, even though he was not the perpetrator of the defiling behavior; he intervened with his identification with the sins of his fathers' household. Nehemiah repented humbly, and it was heard and seen by Yehovah.

If MY People . . .

The Awakening Ekklesia

The time for Christ's Ekklesia to awaken is now.

The Ekklesia must come to life again in the power of Christ's resurrection.

RE-Vival: Something was alive; it became dead and is now alive again. The very meaning of revival says that the Ekklesia needs revival.

We have more authority to change things than we know.

The arising Ekklesia CAN save nations.

The Ekklesia is His government upon the earth. We did not say that the church is His government upon the earth. Although the church plays an

45

essential role in the Kingdom of heaven manifesting upon the earth, the church is not the center of the government of God.

Isaiah prophesied the Messiah's coming, saying,

"For a Child is born; to us, a Son is given; and the government is on His shoulder; and His name is called
Wonderful, Counselor,
The Mighty God,
The Everlasting Father,
The Prince of Peace.
There is <u>no end to the increase</u>
<u>of His government</u> and of peace."[27]

The Ekklesia is Christ's government. His operational government on earth as it is in heaven. Let's look at some things that the Ekklesia does in the world:

Sometime in the late 1980s - early 1990s - I (Wayne) trained intercessors to be the solution instead of complaining about the problem. A pop music artist worked openly in witchcraft on stage as part of his performances. He was coming

---

[27] Isaiah 9:6-7 (LITV)

to our city, and a big concert was being advertised that filled a sports facility. While no one in the churches of the region wanted to go near the place, we purchased concert tickets for five intercessors and sent them in with several decrees for them to make during the concert. They were not sent there to be entertained but to do the works of the Kingdom of heaven. The result was that the electronics of that concert failed to operate, and the show could not take place.

At that time, numerous schools in our area complained about excessive amounts of bullying amongst the students. So, we sent four intercessors, one for each corner of the property at the school, with decrees of heavenly justice and the bullying stopped utterly.

We did a similar plan with several road intersections where repetitive serious accidents happened. The intercessors each stood at the different corners or curves and forcefully spoke the heavenly decrees, and the accidents stopped taking place.

Agnes Sanford[28] was said to have bought a home directly on the San Andres Fault. She did so in response to stop the word of the prophets who said that California would have a new coastline and the wickedness of Hollywood, and the government would be chastised by Yehovah. The House of Agnes Sanford was said to be a house of prayer and repentance.

> *"... But where sin abounded, grace abounded much more, so that as sin reigned in death, even so, grace might reign through righteousness to eternal life through Jesus Christ our Lord."*
> Romans 5:20-21 (NKJV)

When we show up packing our authority on high because we are seated together with Him in Heaven, grace manifests in abounding measures.

Sean Feucht is one of the best examples that can be found. He went

---

[28] Agnes Mary Sanford (November 4, 1897 – February 21, 1982), https://en.wikipedia.org/wiki/Agnes_Sanford

directly into the politics of the State of California and became a light in a very dark place. Then he began his trek throughout the United States to the worst areas with open worship. Change takes place, and evil loses its grip. Being in any of Sean's worship experiences is an exciting adventure.

About a decade ago, I (Wayne) flew to Lima, Peru, with my son Joshua on a miracle mission. We had a long layover in Denver, Colorado, and were sitting in the United Airlines lounge while waiting for our next flight to Houston, Texas. A big-screen television could barely be heard by us playing something quite a distance away from us in the room.

Suddenly, the volume increased on the television, and we came to believe it was supernatural. A man began to speak on the imminent failure of the U.S. Dollar and the failing economy and gave extremely believable facts and figures. We listened intently and heard things explained that we partially knew of and became alarmed by the information showing the fall of the dollar and its economy. When this infomercial was done, the sound went back down to what could barely be heard.

Joshua and I conversed about the economic principles we heard on our trip from Denver to Houston and from Houston to Lima, Peru. When we arrived in Lima, our close friend and colleague, Marco Llinella, met us in the airport terminal, and we went for coffee and waited for other team members to arrive.

While we sat at a table with our coffee, Marco asked us about the U.S. Dollar and what was taking place with the dollar's economy. We, of course, spilled out the garbage that we had been convinced of by the event that took place in Denver. We echoed the facts that we heard in the infomercial. Finally, Marco put his head down upon the table and began to weep from the depths of his being. He cried out that we must pray for the U.S. Dollar and the U.S. economy because it carries the missionaries of the Kingdom and the gospel of Jesus Christ to the ends of the earth, and it cannot fail for their sake.

Joshua and I were stunned and deeply convicted. However actual the facts may have been, what we had heard was not the Truth by the standards of heaven. Nevertheless, we repented and began to fight for the dollar instead of falling to the theories of man. We trained and assigned intercessors to pray for the U.S. Dollar based not on political or patriotic purposes but for the spreading of the gospel of Jesus Christ and the Kingdom of heaven unto the world. We saw the dangers involved should the Dollar fail.

As we humbled ourselves to intercede, repented of the sins of our nation regarding the economy, and sought His face in this matter, we saw the economy flip and begin to become strong, and the U.S. Dollar became more robust than ever. We have found that the Ekklesia is the answer to the economy. And when we stop listening to the reasonings of the world and listen to the heart of the Father for His people, we can change the world together.

*"For just as Jonah became a
sign to the Ninevites,
so will the Son of Man
be to this generation."*
Luke 11:30 (NASB)

Jonah preached the consequences of the sin and graphically told the people of Nineveh what the outcome of their sin would look like. But they repented. What Jonah prophesied did not come to pass. Jonah heroically did what Yehovah told him. But the people repented.

"If My people, on whom My name is called, shall be humbled, and shall pray, and shall seek My face, and shall turn back from their evil ways, then I will hear from heaven, and forgive their sin, and will heal their land."
2 Chronicles 7:14

The Ekklesia is in an identity crisis that needs to be shaken off. Complaining about the depths of sin that encompasses the world has no effect and wastes Kingdom time and energy.

When Yehovah visited Solomon in his chamber, He told of the coming time when His people would turn away from Him and even be in captivity in another land.

The finishing of the temple that Solomon built for Yehovah was the end of another era.

When Yehovah appeared to Solomon in his chamber, it caused a shift upon the earth in that day. Yehovah's message is eternally real and authoritative through every era of time.

We have built our own kingdoms and our own governments and given the precious things of heaven over to the world.

We ought to be humbled by the facts of what we have given away to the world and its agendas to destroy everything that belongs to Yehovah – Jesus Christ.

- We've given governments the rule over us.
- We've given "marriage," the miracle of holy matrimony, over to the state.
- We've given the education of our children over to the ungodly and caused them to be taught the doctrines of demons.
- We've built basilicas as

monuments to our religions
instead of putting our energy and
effort into building up the family
and the home.

This is a short list of things, *"and
things like these,"*[29] we gave away to the
world.

The Ekklesia in all walks of life is
awakened. The Ekklesia is formulating
the operations of the government
authority of the Kingdom of heaven upon
the earth.

The King of all kings is giving those
individuals who will hear what the Spirit
is saying to the Ekklesia plans of victory.

Calling forth exposures of evil and
believing that exposing corruption will fix
the problems has proven inadequate.

The Ekklesia must start the miracles
with a miracle. The miracle of apology.
Then the miracle of forgiveness destroys
the barriers between believers and the
Holy One.

The Shema of Yehovah then opens the
ears of the heart, and the Ekklesia

---

[29] In Galatians 5:21 (LITV), the apostle Paul uses this phrase "and things like
these, of which I tell you beforehand, as I also said before, that the ones
practicing such things will not inherit the kingdom of God."

receives the plans from heaven. Then, the Ekklesia stands up and acts upon the strategies given.[30]

We believe that all of this can be seen in the words Yehovah spoke to Solomon in his chamber.

*"If My people, on whom My name
is called, shall be humbled, and
shall pray, and shall seek My face,
and shall turn back from their
evil ways, then I will hear
from heaven, and forgive their sin,
and will heal their land."*
2 Chronicles 7:14

---

[30] In the Revelation of Jesus Christ, Chapters two & three, the victorious Christ gives instructive messages to 7 different groups of Ekklesia. He repetitively says, "He who has an ear, let him hear what the Spirit says to the Ekklesia." - Revelation 2 & 3

If MY People . . .

The Mystery of His Name - His People

HIS name unfolds the mystery of a people and a household that suddenly exists (but it was not). To unfold this mystery, we need to think along the lines of two becoming one.

"If My people who are called by My name . . ."

The Hebrew more literally says, *"who have my named called upon them."* This may sound like semantics only, but the mystery of the name is more powerful when understood that the "people" have a name, and His name is invoked upon them, and the two become ONE.

Those who are of His household have

His name called upon them. This scriptural principle is most clearly seen in Numbers 6:22-27 and what is called the Aaronic Blessing:

"Then Yehovah spoke to Moses, saying, 'Speak to Aaron and to his sons, saying, "Thus you shall bless the sons of Israel. You shall say to them: Yehovah bless you, and keep you; Yehovah make His face shine on you, And be gracious to you; Yehovah lift up His countenance on you, And give you shalom." 'So they shall invoke My name on the sons of Israel, and I then will bless them.'"

Verse 27 explains that the priests are to *"invoke"* the name of Yehovah upon the children. By so doing, every member of His household becomes marked with the indelible mark of His name. We do this with our children as well as our sons and daughters of the faith. We invoke His magnificent name upon them and call out their names individually in our prayer protocols. We do the same with our ministry partners[31] and those members of our apostolic network.[32] This causes miracle connections to occur, which we find unexplainable but very real.

Revelation 22:1-4 (NASB)

"Then he showed me a river of the water of life, clear as crystal, coming from the throne of God and of the Lamb, in the middle of its street. On either side of the river was the tree of life, bearing twelve kinds of fruit, yielding its fruit every month, and the leaves of the tree were for the healing of the nations. There will no longer be any curse, and the throne of God and of the Lamb will be in it, and His bondservants will serve Him; they will see His face, and His name will be put upon their foreheads."

This revelation of the Lamb - Jesus Christ shows us the marking of His name upon our foreheads.

Abram connected with the Master of

---

[31] Please consider becoming a ministry partner with Wayne & Stephanie: standsure.net/partner

[32] Consider becoming part of our apostolic family. iamtheway.org/join

the universe, saying, *"I have lifted up my hand to Yehovah - Elohim - Elyon, the possessor of heaven & earth."*[33] This was Abram's covenant connection - His name, the Highest of all in the heavens.

In Genesis 17:3, *"Abram fell on his face, and Elohim talked with him."* He told Abram, *"No longer shall your name be called Abram, but your name shall be Abraham, for I have made you the father of a multitude of nations."*[34]

Many sages say that Yehovah (Yod-Hey-Vav-Hey) added the letter "Hey" to Abram and Sarai as a mark of His name so that they became Abraham and Sarah. We believe this shows the importance of having His name declared upon us (even breathed upon us), revealing that the two become ONE. The Hebrew sages consider the "Hey" as His breath and life breathed into Abram and Sarai so that Yehovah's inheritance would spawn nations from the faith that He gave them.

Abram became Abraham, and Sarai became Sarah. The Hebrew sounds like

---

[33] Genesis 14:22
[34] Genesis 17:5

inhale-exhale.

Western tradition generally weakens the action of naming a person, child, business, etc. We tend to search the world to find a name we like, and the meaning has little to do with our choices. The person's destiny (or business) is or should be incorporated in the given name. The best way to do this is to speak to the Holy One and leave it in His loving care. He will take that destiny which is in His great heart and voice it into the heart of the believer, and the name will come forth. It's really that easy.

In the "naming" of Jesus Christ, it is written,

"And she will bear a son, and you shall call His name Jesus, for He shall save His people from their sins."
"Behold! The virgin will conceive in her womb and will bear a son, and they will call His name Emmanuel" (which translated is, God with us)."[35]
Matthew 1:21 & 23 (LITV)

Jesus had His name called upon Him,

---

[35] Isaiah 7:14

and the fullness of Elohim was also called upon Him as Immanuel.

As children of God, we are in His name, and He is in our name. Jesus makes this point perfectly clear when He says,

"Most assuredly, I say to you, he who believes in Me, the works that I do he will do also; and greater works than these he will do because I go to My Father. And whatever you ask in My Name, that I will do, that the Father may be glorified in the Son. If you ask anything in My Name, I will do it."
John 14:12-14 (NKJV)

Now, this mystery is unfolding, and we can see that we are IN His name, and He is IN ours. The two becoming One.

2nd Chronicles 7:14 tells us that His people who have His name called upon them will move in the Spirit to change the world and see the land healed again. We have found that when most people read this rescuing scripture, they tend to focus on the word "pray." We don't see the word pray as the redeeming part. We believe that the most critical phrase to put your faith to work in is *"My people who have My name called upon them,"* as the central liberating principle. Every expression of vindication hinges on His people and no one else.

Yehovah manifested His Presence to Abraham in Genesis 18 and told Abraham about the destruction He decided to display on the cities of Sodom and Gomorrah because of wickedness. Abraham boldly interceded on behalf of those cities, but his defense was on the part of only the righteous people who abode there. Abraham's negotiating intercession came to the Holy One's decision, *"I will not destroy the city for the sake of ten (righteous)."*

Yehovah's own will always have His attention, rescuing Presence and redeeming love.

If MY People... who are called by MY name...

"My name is called upon them" also turns into *"who are called by MY name."* The very promising principle in the

mystery of *"who are called by MY name"* is that we belong to Him, and every power and principality is aware of it.

As believers, we have His name called upon us. We cannot hide His name by false religion pretending humility. His name is a strong tower; the righteous run into it and are made safe.[36]

"For this reason also, God highly exalted Him, and bestowed on Him the name which is above every name, so that at the name of Jesus every knee will bow, of those who are in heaven and on earth and under the earth, and that every tongue will confess that Jesus Christ is Lord, to the glory of God the Father."
Philippians 2:9-11 (NASB)

"If My people, on whom My name is called, shall be humbled, and shall pray, and shall seek My face, and shall turn back from their evil ways, then I will hear from heaven, and forgive their sin, and will heal their land."
2 Chronicles 7:14

---

[36] Proverbs 18:10

What If?

People pray for the country all the time. But they don't take the proper responsibility. His people make the difference, but "God bless America" is not a healing approach, and there are no measurable results.

What if we learned how to pray in a manner that could bring about results?

We see responsibility as our ability to respond. That can mean a lot of things.

What if we responded to the world with all of our heavenly authority?

His people must respond with their God-given abilities. The underlying understanding of the price the Holy One paid to save, heal and deliver us. He didn't stop there, for He raised us up to be in Him and with Him in heavenly places.[37]

The humble will stop their lives (themselves) and intervene by seeking the face of their Heavenly Father. They will then repent and allow the Holy Spirit to reveal the sins defiling the land so that the response is an apology to the Holy Creator and an apology to the land.

What if believers stopped focusing on the bad things and began to focus on the answers from heaven?

The Holy One is listening. That land is listening because it is the hearts of His people being revealed in loving conversation. What if we understood that Yehovah hears us?

What sins have been committed that would bring about the ruling power's wickedness upon the land?

---

[37] Ephesians 2:6

There are four primary biblical defilements of the land and the household:

- Bloodshed
- Idolatry
- Broken Covenant
- Immorality

What if believers apologized with humility for these sins of our fathers[38] that took place upon our lands?[39]

---

[38] Much like Nehemiah repented: Nehemiah chapter one.
[39] Follow along with Wayne & Stephanie as our podcasts will reveal the principles of healing our land. Standsure.net/mypeople

If MY People . . .

Declaring From Heavenlies

Sometimes people get stuck in the humbling process of prayer and their relational position with the Holy One. However, the sacrifice that Jesus Christ made for us has destroyed the grasp and manipulative power of sin. The behavioral law of sin and death no longer prevails, and sin has no control over us.

But sin is too often given a position of authority by religion that holds human behavior in an idolatrous place, above the Holy One and between the believer's heart and the Heart of Jesus.

His name is called upon us, and yet we are humbled by allowing the world's sins to take a higher place of awe than the Presence of the Almighty in us.

There are many applications or types of sin. Still, if sin has any everlasting effects, it is because the behaviors of sin are placed in authority above and between the believer and the Holy One.

John explains this in his epistle as a removal process of whatever blocks our relationship with Jesus Christ when he writes,

"If we say that we have fellowship with Him and yet walk in the darkness, we lie and do not practice the truth, but if we walk in the Light as He Himself is in the Light, we have fellowship with one another, and the blood of Jesus His Son cleanses us from all sin. If we say that we have no sin, we are deceiving ourselves, and the truth is not in us. If we confess our sins, He is faithful and righteous to forgive us our sins and to cleanse us from all unrighteousness. If we say that we have not sinned, we make Him a liar, and His word is not in us."
1 John 1:6-10 (NASB)

Thus, sin is easily removed from a place of authority that is higher than Jesus, and its heart separation ability is destroyed. Thus, "humbled, and shall pray, and shall seek My face, and shall turn back from their evil ways" is becoming to us. Can we not then be humbled, intervene, seek His face, and turn from sin and evil ways in our lives? Then positioning is central to the authoritative place with the Creator of all that exists.

"And you were dead in your trespasses and sins, in which you formerly walked according to the course of this world, according to the prince of the power of the air, of the spirit that is now working in the sons of disobedience. Among them, we, too, all formerly lived in the lusts of our flesh, indulging the desires of the flesh and the mind, and were by nature children of wrath, even as the rest. But God, being rich in mercy, because of His great love with which He loved us, even when we were dead in our transgressions, made us alive together with Christ (by grace you have been saved) and raised us up with Him, and seated us with Him in the heavenly places in Christ Jesus..."
Ephesians 2:1-6 (NASB)

Not only are the Father and the Son dwelling with us and in us, but we are also dwelling with Him and in Him.[40] He has miraculously made us one.

Being *"seated with Him in the heavenly places"* means we are in counsel with Him. Therefore, we must learn to stop our earthly begging, unite with the Holy Ghost, and declare His Kingdom come! His will be done! On earth as in heaven.

Today is the day for believers to awaken and stand as the Ekklesia of the victorious Christ-Messiah.

Let us be one with Him and declare His will for all creation from heaven. We will witness His healing power for our lands.

"If My people, on whom My name is called, shall be humbled, and shall pray, and shall seek My face, and shall turn back from their evil ways, then I will hear from heaven, and forgive their sin, and will heal their land."
2 Chronicles 7:14

---

[40] John 14:17 (NASB) "Spirit of truth, whom the world cannot receive, because it does not see Him or know Him, but you know Him because He abides with you and will be in you."

Some Proclamations

We'd like to give some examples of proclamations. These can be used as models to build from.

"If My people, on whom My name is called, shall be humbled, and shall pray, and shall seek My face, and shall turn back from their evil ways, then I will hear from heaven, and forgive their sin, and will heal their land."
2 Chronicles 7:14

If MY People . . .

Father in heaven, we worship You in our faith in the Blood of the Son, and by our Blood-covered faith, we belong to You, and we will give no other god(s) any place in our lives.

Your name is holy and holds the highest authority of all creation, and Your Name is called upon us. We are your children.

We are humbled by the growing wickedness of the world surrounding us. We are humbled by our sins and the sins of our fathers. Yet, we followed the idols of religion and allowed the fear of man and false wisdom of worldliness to guide us instead of Your Holy Spirit.

We humbly apologize for our choices that were against Your will - Your heart of love for us. Holy Spirit, please assist us in removing any and every obstacle between us. Let us make our connection of love be pure and resistant-free.

Jesus/Yeshua, we seek your face. Let your countenance be directed toward us now.

We know of your faithfulness and your holy justice that forgives us of sins committed on our lands. Forgive us. Forgive our fathers and mothers for the generations of sins against Your will and Your heart.

We desire to open our hearts to hear deeply into our deepest beings - the deep chambers of our hearts.

We exist to love You, Yehovah-Elohim-Elyon (LORD-God-Most High), with all our hearts, our souls, our minds, and our might.

Yehovah, let Your ears hear our voices as those who are Your people - Your children. Your glorious name has been invoked upon us. We belong to Your Bloodline through our faith in the Blood of the Son - Jesus Christ/Messiah.

Now, let the land be exonerated of any guilt and shame of sins committed upon it. Yehovah, we declare your rule and reign upon our land. We proclaim Your will being done upon our land.

Father of lights, You give us freedom and restore all that evil has stolen from us. Our praise for You will continually be in our mouths. Our hearts burst open with love and gratitude for You and what You are doing in our country. Your people - our people - are blessed beyond measure by You! AMEN

Matthew 6:9-13[41]

"Father of us,"
Establish our heritage and Who our Father is. Speak like His children.
"Who is in the heavens,"
Establish His presence in all heavenly realms. His authority permeates the heavens and the quantum realms about us as well as the physical. He is superior to all.
"Your name is set/established here as holy."
His name is invoked upon each of us, His name is our name, and His name is magnificent. His name is His authority upon us. His name is the sanctuary from

---

[41] Authors' translation from "Change the World with Prayer" by Wayne C. Anderson, available from Amazon: standsure.net/changetheworld

which we come to give justice to the world.

"Come! Kingdom of You."

Be manifest! Here and now as we declare the rule and reign of Yehovah. The very substance of the Lord's rule and reign is in the midst of every issue with which we are properly dealing.

"Let be done! The will of You."

The Creator's will, passions, and dreams are formed and accomplished here and now.

"As in heaven - also on the earth!"

The veil between the heavenly throne of Elohim and the earth is penetrated. The Kingdom and Will of the Most High (Elyon) are now existent and manifest in this place upon which we are focused.

"The bread of us daily (idiom about the manna of the wilderness) *give unto us today."*

Every day - this very day - our providence comes from one source only!

Yehovah-Jesus/Messiah is our Provider, and no one else will be able to say that they have given unto us!

"Forgive us our debts, as we also forgive the debtors of ours."

As His children, we have been given the power and authority to forgive sins and to forget the sins of those who have sinned against us. Therefore, we take those sins of individuals, and we rule over them by the might of His Spirit, destroying every sin by the cross of Yeshua, and we will remember those sins no more, as a work of faith.

"And lead us not into temptation,"

Yahweh! He is our Leader! All that we have and all that we are belongs to our Leader, Yahweh! And our steps are ordered by You, Yahweh! So, we totally yield to His will and His ways. There are, therefore, no temptations that we will face by the leadership of Yahweh. He is our Almighty One.

"but deliver us from the evil."

Lord, just as You led the Israelites out from the slavery of Egypt, You will rescue us from the oppressor in the same way! Therefore, our inheritance is in Yahweh and Him alone. He has taken us out of the world's bondage; thus, we will follow His Presence, remain within His Presence, and be liberated by the Almighty One.

"*Because of You is the kingdom and the power and the glory to all the ages (ions).*"

If it were not for You, Oh, Jesus!

We can see Your rule and Your regal reign operating right here.

We can see Your power changing every physical circumstance.

We can see our eternal reign with all its weightiness in the here and now!

"*Amen.*"

The witness says the Great AMEN and the Presence of the Messiah is here with us. We enjoy His presence.

Our Father which art in heaven,
Hallowed be thy name.
Thy kingdom come. Thy will be done in earth, as it is in heaven.
Give us this day our daily bread.
And forgive us our debts, as we forgive our debtors.
And lead us not into temptation, but deliver us from evil
For thine is the kingdom, and the power, and the glory, forever. Amen.
Matthew 6:9-13 (Authorized Version)

Interested in staying up-to-date with "If MY People?"
Check out our Podcasts:
Standsure.net/mypeople

ABOUT THE AUTHORS
Standsure.Net

Wayne & Stephanie Anderson live in Idaho's "New Wine Country," in the western foothills of the Rocky Mountains of Southwest Idaho.

While in Seattle, Wayne spent the early years as a firefighter for the City of Seattle, and for more than 25 years he pastored in South Seattle. Wayne was the 7th president of the Ministerial Fellowship of the USA, originally founded by John G. Lake. Much of Wayne's ministry has been that of an influential national and international leader. He was one of the principal leaders of Seattle Revival Center, which birthed a revival in the mid-1990's, having also been at the epicenter of revivals in Finland, Mexico, Africa and the US.

Through the ministries of Wayne & Stephanie, they have now established churches and ministries in numerous countries and the couple are the Presiding Apostolic Directors of International Apostolic Ministries, a growing apostolic family network.

Wayne and his eldest son Joshua were honorably summoned to appear before the current Sanhedrin in Jerusalem on June 4th, 2013, which was a momentous and life-changing experience.

Wayne periodically speaks with governmental leaders in the United States and other nations with an anointed voice of wisdom, which changes the hearts of leaders.

Wayne & Stephanie write with a growing revelatory development toward fathering and miracles. While they continue to travel the world teaching & equipping believers with keys of the Kingdom of God, they can also be found live on social medias and podcasting from their recording studio on the beautiful Snake River in Southwest Idaho. As authors Wayne & Stephanie diligently work to change the landscape of the Kingdom worldview of believers around the globe.

The responsibility of a nation in peril belongs to His people and not politicians or the media, or any consortium of wealthy plutocrats. His people, however strong or weak they may seem, hold the true destiny of a nation in their hand. When His people call out to Him,
He Heals.

Order "If MY People..." at:
standsure.net/ifmypeople

If MY People . . .

This book investigates one of the greatest mysteries of all time. The great mystery of "Christ in you, the hope of glory." Yet, we desire to see where this mystery begins to unfold and how it takes us to the manifestation of miracles, how the Messiah ministry era began, and how the miracle ministry of the Messiah will increase manifestations upon the earth in coming days.
This is the revelation of the mystery of
one and one becomes ONE!

Order "The Mystery in ONE" at
standsure.net/mystery

If MY People . . .

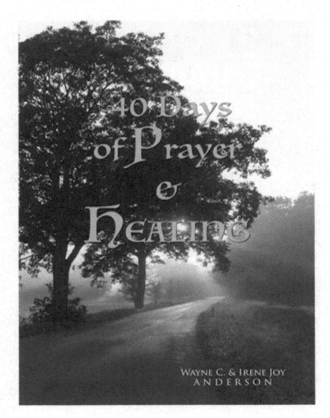

"When a man/woman of integrity prays, angels stop and listen, creation hears the sound, the ear of God is attentive, and all wait to obey the Creator's word on the matter."

The power of prayer is an awesome thing! Wayne & Irene bring you into Yehovah's courts with a real blueprint for victory. Experience the divine healing substance of heaven flow into you and your loved ones with these 40 Days of Prayer & Healing.

Order "40 Days of Prayer & Healing" at standsure.net/40days

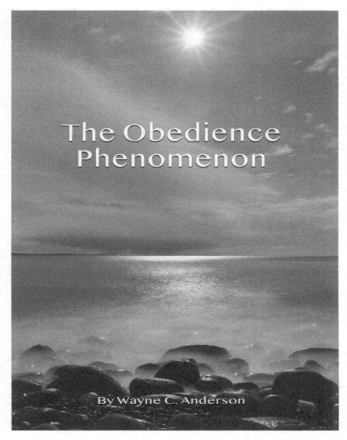

The Obedience
Phenomenon

By Wayne C. Anderson

Dear Reader, My sincere desire in writing this book is several
fold: That you will be able to set a new Kingdom definition into
your heart of what real obedience is. That you will come to
understand that all obedience is accomplished in His Presence.
That you will come to recognize the earthly phenomenons that
take place around you when you are in His Presence.
And, that you will come to know of the numerous portals to
His Presence.

My abiding hope, Wayne C. Anderson

Order "The Obedience Phenomenon" at
standsure.net/obedience

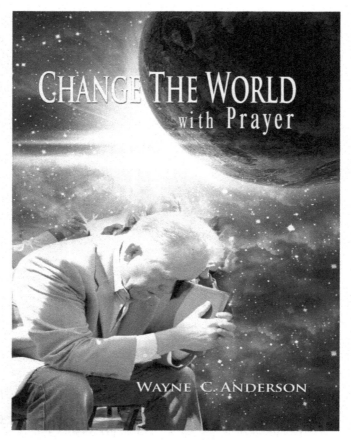

The world is in appalling condition in virtually every aspect. The troubles that surround us are massive, and so overwhelming that it may seem a solution is incomprehensible. We have but one choice...

We must learn to pray as Jesus teaches, and not our own way. The Lord's Prayer is the most dynamic and effective teaching on prayer, and comes from the Master Himself.

Wayne C Anderson, is a revelatory teacher who has put the principles in this book to work for more than four decades of ministry.

This is a book that has answers that will change the world around you.

Order "Change The World With Prayer" at
standsure.net/changetheworld

If MY People . . .

In 1984 Wayne C. Anderson was taken to heaven - the Throne Room of the Lord. He sat on the Father's lap for several hours. The testimony is the extraordinary account of the many wonders of the heaven that he witnessed. This life changing experience will invite the reader into the Presence of the Holy One to witness the many wonders of His love and attention to His believing children. Heaven will become closer than you've ever expected. Home is where the throne of the Father is.

Order: "Home Is Where The Throne Is" at standsure.net/throneroom

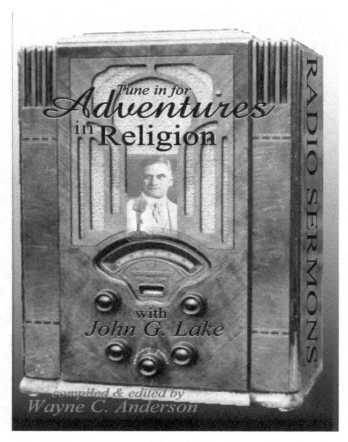

Tune in for *Adventures* in **Religion**

with *John G. Lake*

compiled & edited by
Wayne C. Anderson

RADIO SERMONS

John Graham Lake was a faith filled man at a unique time in the history of the body of Christ upon the earth. In a day when religion reeked with religion of unbelief and Lake was one of the few voices that not only preached the Kingdom messages of the Word of God but he boldly demonstrated the miraculous wonders of the Biblical promises. Lake used the cutting-edge technology of his day and went on the AM Radio in Spokane, Washington to proclaim the miracles of Jesus Christ. This book is a collection of some of those radio program scripts.

Order "Adventures In Religion" at
standsure.net/jglake

If MY People . . .

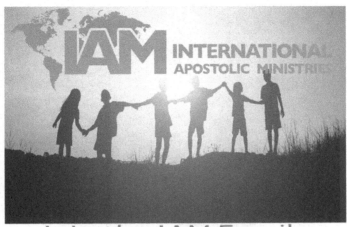

Join the IAM Family
FOR MORE INFORMATION SEE IAMTHEWAY.ORG

IAM is a Family of people who love God,
Churches that are changing thier communitites,
Ministries that are proclaiming the kingdom of Heaven,
Marketplace businesses that operate by the principles of
"Compassionate Capitalism",
and the kind of folks that have a single passion to make
the name of Jesus Christ Famous throughout the earth!
International Apostolic Ministries has always been an
organization of revivalists who have the spiritual DNA
that makes them a tribe of Judah!

For more information see
IAMTHEWAY.ORG

If MY People . . .

Partner Benefits Include:
Regular Partner Revelatory Podcasts
Frequent Revelatory Short-Articles
A Position On Our Prayer Board
Free Entrance into Standsure U Courses of Study
Partner Zoom Meetings with Guest Speakers
Exclusive Partner Website

For more informations see:
Standsure.net/Partner

If MY People . . .